REGARDS...

Françoise Perrot

THE SAINTE-CHAPELLE PARIS

ÉDITIONS DU PATRIMOINE
CENTRE DES MONUMENTS NATIONAUX

SAMARITAINE

INTRODUCTION

"But the most beautiful of chapels, the king's chapel [the Sainte-Chapelle], very conveniently placed within the perimeter of the royal residence, is admired for its very strong structure and for the indestructible solidity of the materials that form it."

Jean de Jandun, *A Treatise of the Praises of Paris*, 1323
Edited and translated by Robert W. Berger, *In Old Paris* (New York: Italica Press, 2002), 8.

Saint Louis, a statue commissioned in about 1307 by Enguerrand de Marigny, a minister of Philippe le Bel (Philip the Fair), for the chapel of his chateau in Mainneville, Eure. It is kept in the church of Saint-Pierre de Mainneville and a cast is on display in the lower chapel (MAP, Charenton-le-Pont).

The Île de la Cité seen from the towers of Notre-Dame: the spire that appears behind the police headquarters, on the right, is that of the Sainte-Chapelle.

Admiration for the Sainte-Chapelle in Paris, as shown by the 14th-century theologian, has not wavered over the centuries and the building is so much a part of the collective imagination that, as late as the 18th century, wine was described as having "the colour of the windows of the Sainte-Chapelle", as the learned Father Lebeuf, historian of the diocese of Paris, observed.

The Sainte-Chapelle is a highly symbolic monument. The personality of its founder, King Louis IX, a Capetian king canonised in 1297, is the main reason for this. Then there is its location at the heart of the royal palace, on the Île de la Cité in Paris, an emblem of temporal power, as a counterpoint to the spiritual power held by the bishop who sat at the neighbouring Notre-Dame Cathedral. Finally, it is an edifice whose sum components—the architecture, sculpture, and stained-glass windows, not to mention the liturgy that provided it with a living—contributed to glorifying the place of the most Christian king in the economy of the medieval world.

Before visiting this distinguished monument as it is today, and to better understand it, it is necessary to step back in time to the 13th century, when it took shape.

Louis IX, Capetian king

The coronation of Louis VIII and Blanche of Castile, the parents of Saint Louis, depicted in the 15th century in *Les Grandes Chroniques de France* (Bibliothèque Municipale, Toulouse, ms. 512, f. 263).

Louis IX was part of the prestigious royal line, founded by Hugues Capet (Hugh Capet) in 987, when it was at its zenith. He would always remember Poissy, where he was born in April 1214, and would sign a number of documents "Louis de Poissy".

His parents were Louis VIII, son of King Philippe Auguste of France, and Blanche of Castile, daughter of King Alfonso VIII of Castile and Eleanor of England.

Blanche was thus the granddaughter of one of the most famous figures of the Middle Ages, Eleanor of Aquitaine, who, at the age of 80, made the journey to Palencia in Castile to choose her as the wife of the future king of France. The episode is portrayed in the stained-glass windows of the Sainte-Chapelle.

Married in 1200, Louis and Blanche only reigned for three years, from 1223 to 1226. Louis VIII pursued the work of his father and died combating the Cathar heresy, after the siege of Avignon. When he felt the end was near, Louis had Queen Blanche recognised as regent of the kingdom. Respecting her husband's wishes, she hastened to have the young Louis IX crowned at Reims on 29 November 1226.

Given the circumstances, one might have thought the succession was far from secure. But since the reign of Philippe Auguste (the byname of King Philippe II, grandfather of Louis IX), the kingdom of France had already occupied an undisputed place in Christendom. Through a series of alliances by marriage and by making skilful use of the feudal system, Philippe Auguste brought together under his control an extensive territory over which he affirmed his domination through direct representatives, the bailiffs. As it was so well-organised, the kingdom of France was one of the richest of its time, circumstances favourable to the future Sainte-Chapelle building project.

The tympanum of the Joshua window illustrates the story of Ruth and Boaz. On this detail, Ruth chooses Boaz for a husband: the scene evokes the choice of Blanche of Castile as the future wife of Louis VIII (MAP, Charenton-le-Pont).

Still considering the affairs of this world, but turning to foreign policy, the rivalry between the kingdom of France and the Empire should be borne in mind. After the division of the Carolingian Empire founded by Charlemagne in 843, the Germanic part inherited the imperial title and became the Holy Roman Empire—which placed the king of France after the emperor. This rivalry focused on the figure of Charlemagne, for whom Philippe Auguste professed a great attachment, which he passed on to his grandson. Emperor Frederick Barbarossa had had the pope canonise Charlemagne in 1164–65. Then, in 1238, Emperor Frederick II made a success of a marketing campaign: he instituted a great procession, at the Palatine Chapel of Aachen, around the reliquary built between 1200 and 1216 to receive the body of Charlemagne. The pilgrimage was to take place every seven years.

These events undoubtedly played a role in the founding of the Sainte-Chapelle in Paris, in which there are many references to the Holy Roman emperor. It would soon give Louis IX the opportunity to increase the prestige of the French monarchy.

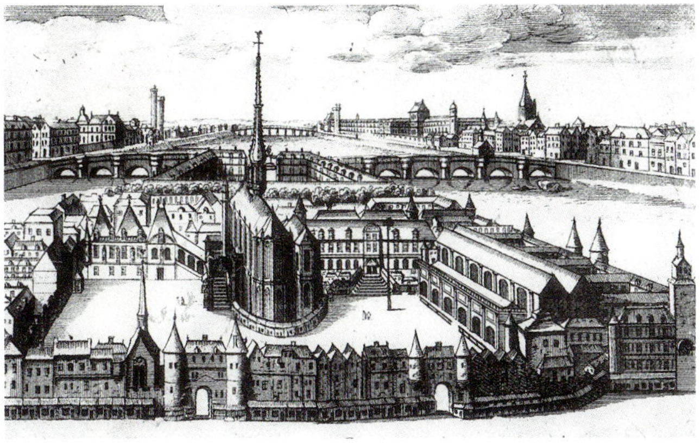

wall, entire sections of which are still visible today. It was also the administrative centre of the kingdom whose various bodies, such as the *Parlement* and the *Chambre des Comptes* (Chamber of Accounts), were located in the old royal palace that Robert le Pieux (Robert the Pious), Hugues Capet's successor, had had built on the Île de la Cité in the 10th century. To house the archives, Louis IX would have built, in addition to the Sainte-Chapelle, a building of the same form but on a smaller scale, called the Trésor des Chartes. It was destroyed in the 18th century.

The palace was thus the principal residence of kings and would remain so for another two centuries.

A view of the Sainte-Chapelle and the Trésor des Chartes in the Cour de Mai in the early 17th century. *Representation of the Palais Royal en la Cité*, by Boisseau, engraving, early 20th century, published in Henri Stein, *Le Palais de Justice et la Sainte-Chapelle de Paris. Notice historique et archéologique* (Paris: D. A. Longuet, 1912), facing page 1.

The king in his Palais de la Cité

As was customary at the time, the king and his entourage moved around the kingdom. When Louis IX succeeded his father, the kingdom was far from being a homogeneous group of territories. Other territories, whose lords were bound to the king of France by feudal ties, consolidated around the royal domain, where the king directly exercised his seigniorial rights.

Against this backdrop of broken-up territories, Paris saw itself attributed a preponderant role during the reign of Philippe Auguste. The city then extended over the two banks of the river and the king had it surrounded with a protective outer

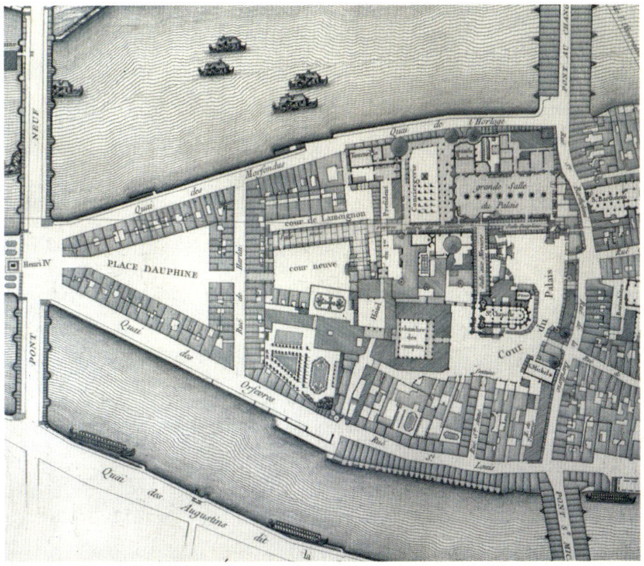

Plan of the tip of the Île de la Cité with the royal palace in 1754. From Jean Delagrive (1689–1757), *Plan détaillé de la Cité dédié à messire Louis Basile de Bernage, conseiller d'État, prévôt des marchands, et à messieurs les échevins de la Ville de Paris*, 1754 (BNF, Paris).

The Church: Notre-Dame Cathedral and the mendicant orders

The other focus of medieval life, the Church, was located on the eastern part of the Île de la Cité. In Paris, the bishop presided over ceremonies in his church, Notre-Dame Cathedral, and lived in the neighbouring episcopal palace. When the king decided to have the Sainte-Chapelle built, the new cathedral—the present edifice rebuilt from 1163 onwards—was still under construction: the arms of the transept were being lengthened.

As an institution, the Church exercised a spiritual magisterium over the secular royal power, through the liturgy and also through the cathedral school, which acted as the guarantor of Christian doctrine. The cathedral school was the embryo of a university in which Philippe Auguste—him again—intervened by giving it the beginnings of recognition. The establishment had little to do with university as we know it. It was a "sworn community", a little like a guild, which brought together masters and students in a network of colleges. The college founded by Robert de Sorbon, Saint Louis' chaplain, later gave birth to the present-day Sorbonne. Intellectual debates were lively and Odo of Châteauroux, the cardinal who would preside over the consecration of the Sainte-Chapelle, declared: "Gaul is the oven in which the intellectual bread of the entire world is baked."

The Stained-Glass Windows of the Sainte-Chapelle by Louis Steinheil, gouache on paper, c. 1850. Two monks bringing relics back from Byzantium. Detail of the so-called Relics window (MAP, Charenton-le-Pont).

Around 1236, the University of Paris authorised a revision of the Bible: the various texts were collected in a single volume, in a format that was easier to handle, and they were put together in an order similar to the current one—the stained-glass windows of the Sainte-Chapelle would adopt it.

The Parisian colleges were much frequented by mendicant friars, that is, the Franciscans and the Dominicans. This new type of monks abandoned the cloisters of monasteries to settle in the towns, which were then rapidly developing demographically and economically, and thus ready to hear their message. They left a profound mark on the society of their time and played a major role alongside Saint Louis.

To understand 13th-century society and its mentality, the importance of the interweaving of religious thought and secular life cannot be overstated.

Louis IX, a crowned king, a just king, a pious king

The king himself combined in his person two components, secular and religious. By birth, he was king, and thus the leader of the affairs of this world. The unction he received during the coronation at Reims then invested him with a supernatural quality. This exceptional dimension brought him closer to the ecclesiastical state while leaving him a layman. The sharing of power between the king and the Church was thus not simple. The programme developed in the Sainte-Chapelle clarified these various aspects.

Louis IX proved to be a particularly pious king, who established a great many religious foundations, such as the abbey of Royaumont or the Hôpital des Quinze-Vingts in Paris, intended to house three hundred blind people and still active today.

His reputation as a just king was equally well-known, and legend has it that he dispensed justice under the oak tree at his Château de Vincennes or in the gardens of his Palais de la Cité.

His participation in the Crusade to the Holy Land would emphasise all these qualities.

Saint Louis washes the feet of the poor and gives food to a leprous monk. Reproductions of two scenes, painted for an altarpiece (?) of the Sainte-Chapelle and now disappeared, for the scholar Nicolas Claude Fabri de Peiresc (1580–1637). Ink and wash on parchment (Bibliothèque Inguimbertine, Carpentras, Archives et Musée du Fonds Peiresc, ms. 1779, fol. 77r and 81r).

The Crusade in the Holy Land

The notion of Crusade was at its peak in the 13th century. It was part of the religious thinking of those with a calling to go on one: it was a duty to God as well as a means of improving oneself spiritually and obtaining the forgiveness of one's sins. It focused mainly on the liberation and defence of the Holy Places, where Christ had lived, particularly Jerusalem, with the Holy Sepulchre (the tomb of Christ).

The region was repeatedly menaced by the Saracens, despite the establishment of principalities governed by Christian princes. Given the events that shook the Holy Land in the first half of the 13th century, it would have been difficult for the future Saint Louis not to have felt the call of the Crusade: the building of the Sainte-Chapelle was part of the king's preparation for this exceptional pilgrimage.

Such was the king preparing to house the major relics of Christendom and to found, in the heart of his Parisian palace, a chapel that would ensure the future Saint Louis and his entire dynasty remarkable fame.

The importance of relics in the Middle Ages

For the man of the Middle Ages, relics played a major role in religious devotion. They guaranteed the oaths taken in their presence and, above all, were the source of miracles. Their nature varied: the most significant were the bodies of those who had died in the odour of sanctity and, by

extension, the objects belonging to them or having been in contact with them.

For Christ and the Virgin Mary, things were more delicate as their bodies had not remained on earth after their deaths. Thus, relics could only be objects associated with them in one way or the other.

The Crown of Thorns

The instruments of Christ's Passion are the objects with the highest symbolic value. They were thus particularly sought after. Some of these great relics had been discovered, if one believes the legend, by Saint Helen, the mother of Emperor Constantine, who imposed the Christian religion on the Roman Empire. It is therefore not surprising that, for the most part, they were deposited in Constantinople, in the chapel of the imperial palace. Since 1204, the Byzantine emperor was a Latin prince from a family close to the Capetian kings.

In 1237, Emperor Baudouin II de Courtenay (Baldwin of Courtenay) was finding it difficult to defend his territory and, seeking subsidies, announced that he intended to part with the most important of the great relics, the Crown of Thorns. This referred to Christ's kingship on earth, that of the king of suffering, as described by John in chapter 13 of his Gospel, a legacy that Louis IX claimed for himself. The king was informed and announced his intention to purchase the Crown of Thorns. His deed had extraordinary repercussions, at first on the religious level. The king and his family headed the procession that brought the Crown to Villeneuve-l'Archevêque, near Sens, Yonne; Louis IX and his brother Robert themselves took care of the burden that they carried to Sens Cathedral.

Repercussions on the political level were no less intense: the arrival of the Crown of Thorns, the purest symbol of royalty, made the kingdom of France the chosen land of Christendom, which thus found itself to be the equal of the Holy Roman Empire.

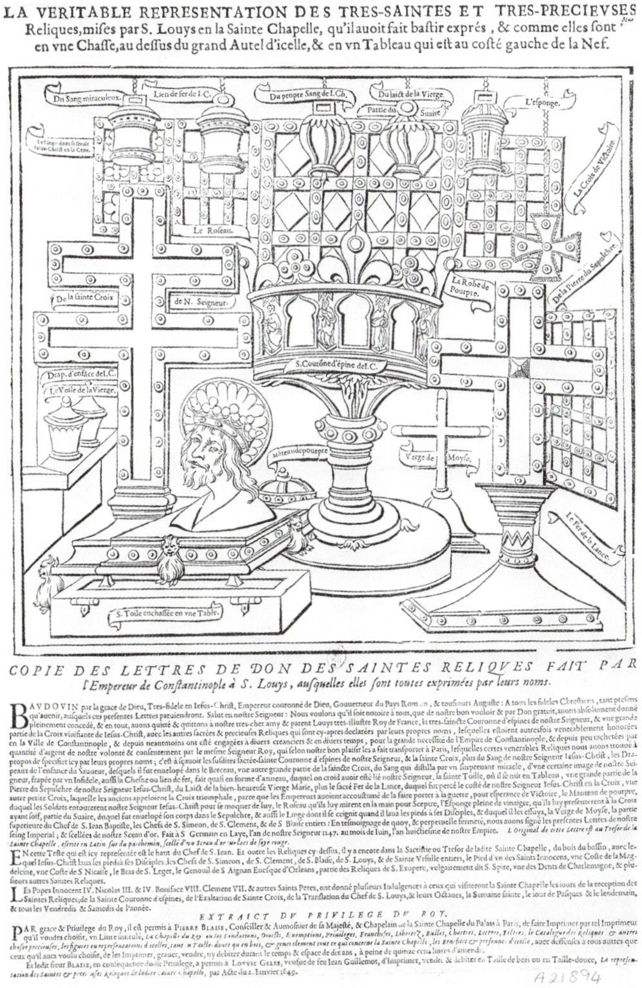

LA VERITABLE REPRESENTATION DES TRES-SAINTES ET TRES-PRECIEVSES Reliques, mises par S. Louys en la Sainte Chapelle, qu'il auoit fait bastir exprés, & comme elles sont en vne Chasse, au dessus du grand Autel d'icelle, & en vn Tableau qui est au costé gauche de la Nef.

COPIE DES LETTRES DE DON DES SAINTES RELIQVES FAIT PAR l'Empereur de Constantinople à S. Louys, ausquelles elles sont toutes exprimées par leurs noms.

BAVDOVIN par la grace de Dieu, Tres-fidele en Iesus-Christ, Empereur couronné de Dieu, Gouuerneur du Pays Rom[illegible], & tousiours Auguste : A tous les fideles Chrestiens, tant presens qu'auenir, ausquels ces presentes Lettres paruiendront. Salut en nostre Seigneur : Nous voulons qu'il soit notoire à tous, que de nostre bon vouloir & par Don gratuit, auons absolument donné pleinement concedé, & en tout, auons quitté & quittons à nostre tres-cher amy & parent Louys tres-illustre Roy de France, la tres-saincte Couronne d'espines de nostre Seigneur, & vne grande partie de la Croix viuifiante de Iesus-Christ, auec les autres sacrées & precieuses Reliques qui sont cy-apres declarées par leurs propres noms, lesquelles estoient autresfois venerablement honorées en la Ville de Constantinople, & depuis neantmoins ont esté engagées à diuers creanciers & en diuers temps, pour la grande necessité de l'Empire de Constantinople, & depuis peu rachetées par quantité d'argent de nostre volonté & consentement par le mesme Seigneur Roy, qui selon nostre bon plaisir les a fait transporter à Paris, lesquelles certes venerables Reliques nous auons troué à propos de specifier icy par leurs propres noms ; c'est à sçauoir les susdites sacrée-sainte Couronne d'espines de nostre Seigneur, & la sainte Croix, plus du Sang de nostre Seigneur Iesus-Christ, les Drapeaux de l'enfance du Sauueur, desquels il fut enuelopé dans le Berceau, vne autre grande partie de la saincte Croix, du Sang qui distilla par vn surprenant miracle, d'vne certaine image de nostre Seigneur, frapée par vn Infidele, aussi la Chesne ou lien de fer, fait quasi en forme d'anneau, duquel on croid auoir esté lié nostre Seigneur, la sainte Toille, où il se mit en Tableau, vne grande partie de la Pierre du Sepulchre de nostre Seigneur Iesus-Christ, du Laict de la bien-heureuse Vierge Marie, plus le sacré Fer de la Lance, duquel fut percé le costé de nostre Seigneur Iesus-Christ en la Croix, vne autre petite Croix, laquelle les anciens appeloient la Croix triomphale, parce que les Empereurs auoient accoustumé de la faire porter à la guerre, pour esperance de Victoire, le Manteau de pourpre, duquel les Soldats entourerent nostre Seigneur Iesus-Christ pour se moquer de luy, le Roseau qu'ils luy mirent en la main pour Sceptre, l'Esponge pleine de vinaigre, qu'ils luy presenterent à la Croix ayant soif, partie du Suaire, duquel fut enuelopé son corps dans le Sepulchre, & aussi le Linge dont il se ceignit quand il laua les pieds à ses Disciples, & duquel il les essuya, la Verge de Moyse, la partie superieure du Chef de S. Iean Baptiste, les Chefs de S. Simeon, de S. Clement, & de S Blaise entiers : En tesmoignage de quoy, & perpetuelle fermeté, nous auons signé les presentes Lettres de nostre seing Imperial ; & scellées de nostre Sceau d'or. Fait à S Germain en Laye, l'an de nostre Seigneur 1247. au mois de Iuin, l'an huictiesme de nostre Empire. *L'Original de cette Lettre est au Tresor de la Sainte Chapelle, escrite en Latin sur du parchemin, scellé d'vn Sceau d'or sur lacs de soye rouge.*

EN cette Teste qui est icy representée est le haut du Chef de S. Iean. Et outre les Reliques cy-dessus, il y a encore dans la Sacristie ou Tresor de ladite Sainte Chapelle, du bois du bassin, auec lequel Iesus-Christ laua les pieds à ses Disciples, les Chefs de S. Simeon, de S. Clement, de S. Blaise, de S. Louys, & de Sainte Vrsulle entiers, le Pied d'vn des Saints Innocens, vne Coste de la Magdeleine, vne Coste de S Nicaise, le Bras de S. Leger, le Genouil de S Aignan Euesque d'Orleans, partie des Reliques de S. Exupere, vulgairement dit S. Spire, vne des Dents de Charlemagne, & plusieurs autres Saintes Reliques.

LEs Papes Innocent IV. Nicolas III. & IV. Boniface VIII. Clement VII. & autres Saints Peres, ont donné plusieurs Indulgences à ceux qui visiteront la Sainte Chapelle les iours de la reception des Saintes Reliques; de la Sainte Couronne d'espines, de l'Exaltation de Sainte Croix, de la Translation du Chef de S. Louys, & leurs Octaues, la Semaine sainte, le iour de Pasques & le lendemain, & tous les Vendredis & Samedis de l'année.

EXTRAICT DV PRIVILEGE DV ROY.

PAR grace & Priuilege du Roy, il est permis à PIERRE BLAISE, Conseiller & Aumosnier de sa Majesté, & Chapelain de la Sainte Chapelle du Palais à Paris, de faire Imprimer par tel Imprimeur qu'il voudra choisir, vn Liure intitulé, *La Chapelle du Roy en ses Fondations, Droicts, Exemptions, Priuileges, Franchises, Libertez, Bulles, Chartres, Lettres, Tiltres, le Catalogue des Reliques & autres choses precieuses, les figures ou representations d'icelles, tant en Taille-douce qu'en bois, & generalement tout ce qui concerne la Sainte Chapelle, les Benefices & personnes d'icelle*, auec deffenses à tous autres que ceux qu'il aura voulu choisir, de les Imprimer, grauer, vendre, ny debiter durant le temps & espace de dix ans, à peine de quinze cens liures d'amende.

Et ledit sieur BLAISE, en consequence dudit Priuilege, a permis à LOVYSE GELEE, veufue de feu Iean Guillemot, d'Imprimer, vendre & debiter en Taille de bois ou en Taille-douce, *La representation des Saintes & precieuses Reliques de ladite Sainte Chapelle*, par Acte du 2. Ianvier 1649.

The Life and Miracles of Saint Louis by Guillaume de Saint-Pathus, illumination on parchment, c. 1330–40. Saint Louis in prayer at the Sainte-Chapelle (BNF, Paris, Mss, ms. fr. 5716, f. 67).

The True Representation of the Most-Holy and Most-Precious Relics, Placed in the Sainte Chapelle by St Louys. Woodcut, 1649 (BNF, Paris, Est. Et Phot., Va 225 F, no. 2184).

The Stained-Glass Windows of the Sainte-Chapelle by Louis Steinheil, gouache on paper, c. 1850. Saint Louis and his brother Robert d'Artois carry the relics. Detail of the so-called Relics window (MAP, Charenton-le-Pont).

View of the treasury of the Sainte-Chapelle in the missal of the Duke of Bedford (c. 1424–32), f. 83v. Gouache copy on parchment executed in 1837 (Musée National du Moyen Âge-Thermes de Cluny, Paris, Cl. 22847).

Translation of the reliquary containing the head of Saint Louis in 1306. *Missal* of the Sainte-Chapelle. Miniature on parchment, after 1503 (BNF, Paris, Mss, ms. lat. 8890, fo 21).

The treasury

In 1241, still in search of money, Emperor Baudouin sold to Louis IX other exceptional relics kept in Constantinople. These included, first, two fragments of the Cross on which Christ had been crucified: one was named the True Cross, the other the Cross of Victory. To these were added other relics of the Passion—such as the Holy Sponge (which the executioner offered to the dying Christ), the lance with which the centurion Longinus had pierced Christ's side, and a fragment of the Holy Shroud, the cloth with which Christ's body was wrapped after his death—as well as the head of Saint John the Baptist, those of Saint Clement and Saint Blaise, etc. In all, Saint Louis had twenty-two relics in his possession in 1242, the list of which was confirmed by the formal letter of Baudouin in 1247.

Objects related to the liturgy were added to the treasury. Inventories drawn up by successive treasurers when they took office included liturgical books, ornaments, and vestments, all objects required to celebrate the Holy Offices.

The treasury after the canonisation of Saint Louis

Louis IX died near Tunis in 1270 and his body was brought back to Saint-Denis, the royal necropolis. After the canonisation of his grandfather in 1297, King Philippe IV le Bel (Philip the Fair) had the saintly king's head removed to add to the treasury of the Sainte-Chapelle. The prestige of the chapel was thus reinforced: on a symbolic level, it became the "head" of the kingdom of France.

The treasury of relics was the property of the king, who had an absolute right over it. Saint Louis himself had removed thorns from the Crown of Thorns to give them to allied princes or religious orders he hoped to encourage.

His successors acted in the same fashion. The wood of the True Cross was particularly sought after. Thus, Queen Marie-Thérèse, the wife of Louis XIV, obtained a fragment for her son, the duke of Anjou, in 1672. In 1749, Louis XV authorised the removal of a piece for the consecration of the chapel of the chateau in Choisy-le-Roi that he gave to the Marquise de Pompadour. It was thus to house this exceptional treasure that Louis IX decided to build the Sainte-Chapelle in the heart of his palace in Paris.

The beginnings of the foundation

It is very difficult to say on precisely what date the king decided to build the chapel. The bull from Pope Innocent IV dated 24 May 1244 implied that work was already underway. The building project was probably very advanced in January 1246 since a college of ecclesiastics, responsible for prayers and looking after the relics, was founded.

The third certain date is 25 April 1248: the Sainte-Chapelle was consecrated in the presence of the papal legate Cardinal Odo of Châteauroux, mentioned above for his links to the university, and thirteen other prelates. Thus, on this date, the work on the main structure, and most of the decoration, was finished.

The sick king in Pontoise in 1244. *Le Livre des faits de Monseigneur saint Louis.* Miniature on parchment, c. 1480 (BNF, Paris, Mss, ms. fr. 2829, f. 19v).

A crucial date: the decision to take up the cross (December 1244)

Around the late 1230s, a certain unrest arose in the west of the kingdom: King Henry III of England, with the support of local barons, attempted to win back the former Plantagenet domains that Philippe Auguste had passed to the French crown. Louis IX defeated this coalition at Taillebourg and Saintes (July 1242). However, the trying military campaign had weakened his health and, in December 1244, he had such a serious relapse that it was thought he would not survive. It was during his illness that he decided to take up the cross, that is, to set off on a Crusade to the Holy Land.

This decision is essential to our understanding of the programme developed at the Sainte-Chapelle, whose construction was part of the preparations for the Crusade.

The first foundation (January 1246)

The goal of a first charter, dated January 1246, was to give statutes to the Sainte-Chapelle. A long preamble, which took up nearly half the document, made clear the spirit in which was established the foundation that the king wanted to make part of the dynastic continuity.

For the Sainte-Chapelle was founded first and foremost to save the souls of all the members of the royal family, both the king's predecessors and his entourage. Only then are mentioned the relics of the Passion, and the Crown of Thorns and the Cross in particular. Their presence justified the royal act: they were considered the guardians (the palladium) of the dynasty and the kingdom.

The arrangements for the functioning of the Sainte-Chapelle were made later. The most important ones concerned the college of clerics that the king set up to look after his foundation. However, it must not be forgotten that the Sainte-Chapelle was first and foremost a symbol of the kingdom, a ceremonial chapel of sorts. The daily services the kings attended took place in private chapels and were celebrated by the clerics of his immediate entourage: his confessor and his chaplains, who also accompanied him on his journeys.

The clerics in charge of the divine service

A college of seventeen clerics (ten priests and seven deacons) had to ensure that the divine service was celebrated every day. When the king came to the Sainte-Chapelle, it was his chaplain who officiated.

The text established the list of financial resources allocated to the keep of the ecclesiastical personnel, and went into detail. We thus learn that a supplement of three deniers was attributed to the chaplain who would sleep in the Sainte-Chapelle to look after the treasury of relics. The cost of candles is also mentioned as three candles weighing three pounds were to be permanently lit near the treasury.

Moreover, certain revenues were explicitly allocated for the upkeep of the stained-glass windows, for which the clerics were responsible. This arrangement would be important during the restoration of the large rose window in the late 15th century.

The second foundation (August 1249)

On 29 August 1248, in Aigues-Mortes, before setting off for the Holy Land, the king added to the instructions he had previously given. The financial aspects were confirmed and developed. The principal modification concerned the organisation of the group of priests in charge: one of them was appointed superior of this college of clerics; given that he ensured the duties of guarding the treasury, he was given the title of treasurer. A new hierarchy was thus introduced in the group of clerics, who were called canons from 1303.

For its part, the relationship between the Sainte-Chapelle and the ecclesiastical authorities was not determined until 1304 by a bull from Pope Benedict XI. On the spiritual level, the Sainte-Chapelle came under the direct authority of the Holy See. In any case, because of its presence in the royal palace enclosure, it benefited from the privilege attached to the French crown, which exempted all religious establishments located inside the palace from the control of the bishop of Paris and the archbishop of Sens. It was the king who appointed the members of the ecclesiastical college.

The third foundation (June 1318)

By the letters of June 1318, King Philippe V le Long (Philip the Tall), great-grandson of Saint Louis, increased the ecclesiastical personnel, which numbered forty-three, including five new chaplains. This number remained stable until the closing of the Sainte-Chapelle in 1787.

The cantor in charge of the music and the proper execution of the chants is only mentioned in the texts from 1319–20. And yet music was part of the services and must have been present beforehand. The same remark holds for the masters of the choirboys, mentioned only from 1299—there were eight of them when the chapel closed in 1787.

The temporal—all of the revenues managed by the college of canons—developed until about the 16th century, thanks to the royal donations and various gifts from private individuals, so much so that the Sainte-Chapelle was a major landowner beyond the city limits of Paris. And yet financial difficulties, which would become even more of a burden, were to be one of the causes of the chapel's closure.

As the functioning of the college of canons tended to become lax from time to time, the kings deemed it necessary to intervene on several occasions to impose "reformations", thus demonstrating a constant interest in their forebear's foundation.

The Trésor des Chartes

The foundation of the Sainte-Chapelle was complemented a few years later with the construction of a building, meant to house, on the one hand, the sacristies necessary for the liturgy and, on the other, the archives of the kingdom. This last function led to it being named the Trésor des Chartes (the Treasury of Charters).

Located on its north side, its structure was similar to that of the Sainte-Chapelle, but it was smaller in size. The sacristies communicated with the chapel via doors located in the first north bay of the apse.

In addition to the usual divine service and the great annual ceremonies focussing on the relics of the Passion, the Sainte-Chapelle was the setting for some exceptional events.

The coronation of Queen Marie of Brabant in the Sainte-Chapelle, from *Grandes Chroniques de France* by Jean Fouquet, miniature on parchment, c. 1455–60 (BNF, Paris, Mss, ms. fr. 6465, f° 292).

Two queens of France were crowned there: Marie of Brabant, the second wife of Philippe III le Hardi (Philip the Bold), the son and heir of Saint Louis, on 24 June 1275, and Jeanne of Évreux, the third wife of Charles IV le Bel (Charles the Fair), on 11 May 1326.
Several sovereigns, such as the former Queen Christina of Sweden in 1656, asked to visit the Sainte-Chapelle.
Moreover, the Sainte-Chapelle was also the setting for meetings affecting the life of the kingdom—in 1408, for example, when the assembly of prelates decided to free itself from obedience to the pope.
The canons also headed the most prestigious processions, such as the death of Charles VII in 1461 and that of Louis XI in 1483.

Difficult times

The upkeep of the monument presented recurrent difficulties as may be seen in the accounts. On at least two occasions, vigorous interventions were required.
First, towards the late 15th century, King Charles VIII was alarmed that, if a rapid solution was not found, "the walls, vaults, machicolations, and other elements of the Sainte-Chapelle could go to ruin" (Archives Nationales, LL 610, fol. 121v; cited by Henri Stein, *Le Palais de Justice et la Sainte-Chapelle de Paris. Notice historique et archéologique* [Paris: D. A. Longuet, 1912], 121–22). In January 1485, he ordered that the canons be paid all that was owed to them in terms of income on the domain to allocate it to repairs. The restoration that followed mainly concerned the western side of the building with the large rose window reconstructed in the Flamboyant Gothic style that we now admire.
On 26 July 1630 a terrible fire destroyed the roof with the spire. As the canons were afraid that the fire might reach the large reliquary housing the relics, the locks were forced and the relics moved for safekeeping in the sacristy. The divine service took place in the lower chapel until the month of March 1631. The repairs were carried out slowly and, when Louis XIII came to hear the mass on 18 January 1633, the treasurer presented him with another request for financial aid for repairs.
Another major fire took place on 11 January 1776 in the buildings of the palace without damaging the Sainte-Chapelle. As a result, the Palais de Justice was rebuilt. The installation of the archives, saved in extremis, in new premises condemned the Trésor des Chartes building, which was demolished in 1782–83. A wing of the new Palais de Justice took its place north of the Sainte-Chapelle.

Closed by King Louis XVI

Noting the growing disorganisation, the King's Council declared, by a decision of 11 March 1787, the "suspension" of the Sainte-Chapelle (and other Saintes Chapelles, such as that of Vincennes).
Canon Sauveur Jérôme Morand, a witness of these events, put the royal decision down to the slackening behaviour of the

ecclesiastic personnel and to their incessant disagreements. But above all, "the College de la Ste Chapelle . . . found itself exhausted by the weight of its costs, and the reparation of its buildings, that there remained no other resources to stop its ruin and destruction" (Sauveur Jérôme Morand, *Histoire de la Sainte-Chapelle royale du Palais* [Paris: Clouzier et Prault, 1790], 240). He decided to save the memory of the Sainte-Chapelle, to which he was sincerely attached, by bringing together all the documents concerning it.

In fact the Sainte-Chapelle had had its day as an institution, a victim of the changing times and the rationalism of the Enlightenment.

Project for the Sainte-Chapelle by Félix Duban, pen-and-ink drawing on paper, *c.* 1837 (MAP, Charenton-le-Pont).

Ste-Chapelle, main façade; 15th-century spire by Félix Duban, pen-and-ink drawing on paper, 1837 (?) (MAP, Charenton-le-Pont).

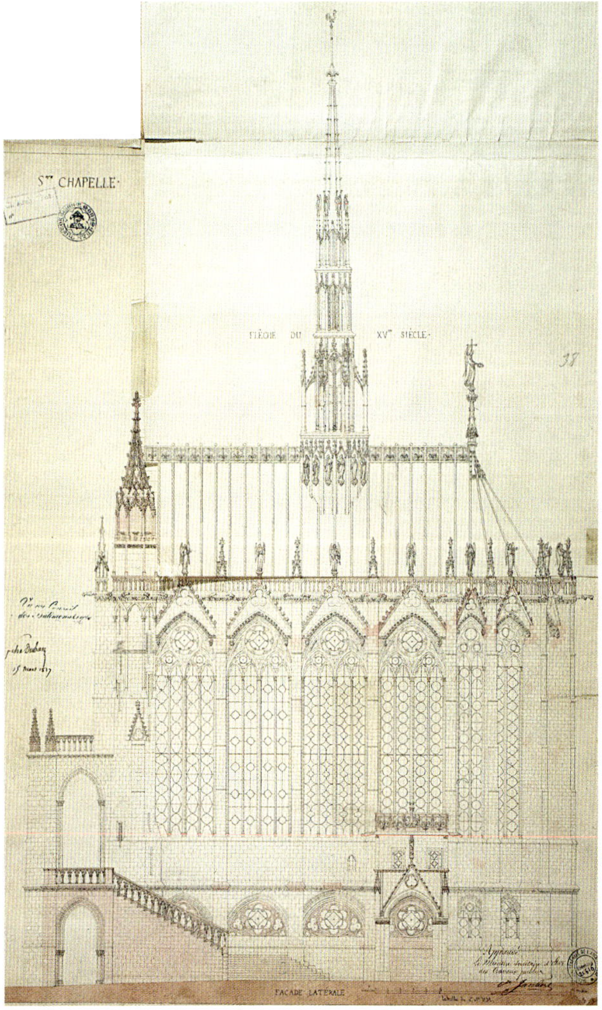

From the Revolution to the July Monarchy

In 1790 the future was bleak: on 4 June, *La Chronique de Paris* noted that "people are busy tearing the lead off the Sainte-Chapelle". It was definitively closed on 22 November 1790 and the college of canons dissolved. In 1791 Louis XVI took the decision to transfer the great reliquary and other reliquaries to Saint-Denis and the books to the royal library.

In 1793 the spire was torn down, two of the three bells sold, and the sculptor François Daujon (1759–c. 1844) was put in charge of destroying the "signs of feudalism"—the emblems that recalled the royal presence—for example, "the arms of France with crowns, collars, and ribbons, above the door . . . forty-two crowns on the panelling of the interior of the chapel, cleanly so as not to damage the panelling" (Archives Nationales, F13 212; cited by Henri Stein, *Le Palais de Justice et la Sainte-Chapelle de Paris. Notice historique et archéologique*, 127).

As luck would have it, the building itself was not demolished. Used as a meeting room by a revolutionary club, then as a flour warehouse, it eventually became an archives' storage for the neighbouring Palais de Justice in 1802–03.

Despite the damage, the Sainte-Chapelle had made it through the revolutionary period relatively unscathed.

The 19th-century restoration (1836–63)

The Sainte-Chapelle owes its current appearance to the great restoration carried out between 1836 and 1863. The administrative body in charge of overseeing the works was the Conseil des Bâtiments Civils, in which there were two opposing aesthetic movements. The first saw itself as the successor of the neoclassicism inherited from the 18th century. The second had a growing interest in all things pertaining to the Middle Ages. The scholars, archaeologists, and historians had found matter for study in the repositories to which the revolutionary seizures had added objects of all sorts, including fragments of architecture, from 1790. In this same movement, a resolutely nationalist history was beginning to be written. After the publication in 1831 of *Notre-Dame de Paris* (*The Hunchback of Notre-Dame*), the famous novel by Victor Hugo, the taste for the Middle Ages was well-established.

In 1835 the observations on the Sainte-Chapelle collected by the architect Jean-Baptiste Lassus (1807–1857) constituted, as it were, a call for its restoration. In fact, the restoration was launched the following year. The first step consisted of carrying out a study with a view to a precise project. It was entrusted to the architect Félix Duban (1798–1870), who was assisted by Lassus, as "first inspector of the works on the Sainte-Chapelle", then by Eugène Viollet-le-Duc (1814–1879), as second inspector.

The office in charge of the restoration of the Sainte-Chapelle thus became a place of particularly rich interaction where the direction of the project was discussed. The main problem: should the monument be restored to the state that was thought to be its original condition? For the architecture as a whole it was possible, but for the decoration—paintings and polychromy, sculpture, stained-glass windows—less easy to find, choices had to be made.

The search for the original condition, or the so-called original condition, that marked the restoration of the Sainte-Chapelle, had repercussions well beyond the project. Viollet-le-Duc made himself its advocate in his publications, particularly in his *Dictionnaire raisonné de l'architecture française du* XIe *au* XVIe *siècle*, published in 10 volumes from 1854 to 1868.

*

The Sainte-Chapelle before the Fire of 1630, engraving by Charles Nicolas Ransonnette, frontispiece for Sauveur Jérôme Morand, *Histoire de la Sainte-Chapelle royale du Palais* (Paris: chez Clousier et Prault, 1790).

The restoration of the Sainte-Chapelle, sometimes harshly criticised, has the merit of having handed down to us a monument that remains a jewel of Rayonnant Gothic architecture.

A double chapel

The general arrangement chosen for the structure is that of a building with two superimposed levels. The lower floor, dedicated to the Virgin Mary, was accessible to the palace personnel. The upper floor, dedicated to the Holy Cross, was principally reserved for the king and his family; it communicated with his apartments. This arrangement reflects the place of the sovereign in the organisation of the world, halfway between his people on earth and God in heaven.

The construction used and developed the technical achievements experimented with on the many building projects undertaken for over a century. The result is a miracle of equilibrium and elegance whose architect unfortunately remains unknown. Various names have been proposed, particularly that of Pierre de Montreuil, who worked on the abbey church (now cathedral) of Saint-Denis and the abbey of Saint-Germain-des-Prés (refectory and chapel of the Virgin, destroyed in the 19th century). But architectural historians tend to reject him out of hand, without coming up with any acceptable alternatives.

The exterior approach

Seen from the exterior, the Sainte-Chapelle presents a rather compact mass as a result of the absence of the flying buttresses usually associated with Gothic constructions. Here, to ensure the stiffening of the walls and buttress the springing of the vaults, sixteen counterforts punctuate the perimeter of the building. They correspond to the bays structuring the interior volumes.

Very thick at ground level, they narrow by successive steps as they climb to the base of the roof where they are topped by pinnacles. A more projecting cornice marks the horizontal separation between the two chapels, lower and upper. The windows ornament the masonry between the counterforts with openwork. The windows of the lower chapel, shaped like curvilinear triangles, were restored by Lassus. We see that those of the upper chapel, with four lancets in the nave and with two lancets in the choir, take the place of the walls.

To the west, the buttressing was provided by the two floors of the porch and, not visible at first glance, by the counterforts hidden by the two staircase turrets.

The roof was entirely redone in the 1850s, at the same time as the spire.

The engraving reproduced by Canon Morand shows the state of the chapel before the fire of 1630. On the south flank appeared the staircase rebuilt around 1500 by King Louis XII, which gave access, from the exterior, to the upper chapel; it was used by the authorised dignitaries, while the members of the royal family entered by the first floor of the porch, on the north side. Very damaged over the centuries, what remained of it was definitively removed by Lassus in 1849–50. The various studies proposed by Duban were not pursued.

At the base of the monument and all around it appeared small buildings where various craftsmen—parchment merchants, goldsmiths, booksellers, etc.—exercised their trade, which led to many everyday annoyances. In 1527 King François I had asked for them to be destroyed, a demand that was repeated several times, which proves that it had never entered into force.

Section Showing the Two Superimposed Levels, engraving by Charles Nicolas Ransonnette, for Sauveur Jérôme Morand, *Histoire de la Sainte-Chapelle royale du Palais* (Paris: chez Clousier et Prault, 1790).

The lower chapel

The portal that gave access to the lower chapel was largely reworked in the 1850s and only a few columns of the embrasure with their capitals belonged to the original building. The initial iconography of the tympanum was uncertain but, as the lower chapel was dedicated to the Virgin, the restorers commissioned a *Coronation of the Virgin* for the tympanum and a *Virgin and Child* for the pier from the studio of the sculptor Adolphe Victor Geoffroy-Dechaume (1816–1892).

The structure of the lower chapel was designed to serve as a base for the upper chapel. It thus has the same length and width, but its plan is different: the nave of four bays, each on a square plan, ends towards the east with a seven-sided chevet and the whole is surrounded by a very narrow ambulatory.

The lower chapel suffered in the terrible flood of the winter of 1690. The floodwaters damaged the tombs of the canons, most of whom were buried in the lower chapel. The engraving by Charles Nicolas Ransonnette (1793–1877) represents the state after the repairs that Canon Morand comments on in his book. The layout of the altars was modified: the main altar was pushed towards the back of the choir and four others (of the six existing ones) were set against the side walls—one of them may be seen on the left of the engraving. A grille was installed to separate the choir from the nave. On the south side (to the right on the document), one can make out frames with clear glass: they close the openings whose old glass had been removed as well as the "stone compartments that diminished the daylight". On the other hand, the north wall has not been modified.

"High and low benches for the College, when it celebrates the Service in the lower-Sainte-Chapelle" were located in the choir. They are not visible on the image, nor is the entrance of the new tomb, placed under an arch near the main altar, for the inhumation of the canons.

In 1802–03, when the Sainte-Chapelle was transformed into an archive for the neighbouring Palais de Justice, cupboards were placed along the walls. They were removed during the 19th century so the lower chapel could be restored to what was assumed to be its original state: this is the present decoration. The only fragment of old painting,

discovered in 1849, is an *Annunciation*, painted directly on the wall in the 13th century, at the north entrance of the choir. The rest of the polychromy was an invention by the restorers who gave a predominant role to heraldic colours: the azure with gold fleurs-de-lis for France and the *gules* (red in heraldic language) with gold castles of Castile for Castile, the homeland of the queen mother, Blanche. The windows framed by curvilinear triangles were restored in the nave, on the south side.
In the north and south corners, on either side of the Western façade, were located the bottom of the staircases that gave access to the upper floor.

The upper chapel: plan and structure

The architecture of the upper chapel features a unified volume with impressive dimensions: 33 metres long by 10.7 metres wide and, especially, 20.5 metres high under the vaults of the nave. These are dimensions worthy of a cathedral—the choir of Noyon Cathedral, for example, is the same height. The nave comprises four bays with rectangular plans that end, in the east, with a seven-sided apse.
What strikes the visitor the most is the abundance of light that comes through the glass placed in the immense windows with four lancets in the nave and two lancets in the choir. The masonry is limited to the strong piers that support the vaults and the wall located at the base of the windows. The design of its architecture makes the upper chapel resemble a huge reliquary.
The upper chapel appears to be the reflection on earth of the Heavenly Jerusalem announced in the Book of Revelation. The polychromy contributes greatly to this impression. All the decoration that glorifies the architecture helps put across a complex message, focussing on two key ideas: the Christian faith and its defence, on the one hand, and the place of the king of France in the world economy, on the other.
To attempt to read this message, there remain the stained glass, the sculpture, and the painting still in situ. The relics gallery, the only surviving artefact, is a reminder of the ceremonies held in the Sainte-Chapelle.

The relics gallery

The relics, the reason for the foundation, were placed in a large reliquary at the back of the choir. The gallery, which overhangs the altar, was built after the consecration of 1248, but before 1267, when Jean de Joinville mentioned them in his *Histoire de Saint Louis* (ed. Albert Pauphilet and Edmond Pognon [Paris: Gallimard, 1952], 360).

Although it had been broken up during the Revolution, Duban and Lassus decided to rebuild this major element of the decoration using salvaged fragments. They were inspired by various documents, including Ransonnette's engraving.

On Good Friday, the king, dressed in his royal vestments, went up to the gallery and himself displayed the True Cross for adoration by the congregation. His successors continued this custom.

The stained-glass windows throughout the ages

Much of the fame of the Sainte-Chapelle is due to its stained-glass decoration. The colourful windows fulfil their role as the wall between the outside world and the religious space, in accordance with 13th-century aesthetics. Each window is divided into lancets—two in the choir, four in the nave—and each of these comprises scenes of various sorts framed by a metal structure.

The harmonious effect of this group should not deceive us: it is the result of the well thought-out choices of the restorers of

the 19th century. When they began this part of the building project, they found stained-glass windows very much altered by successive repairs of variable quality. While certain repairs demonstrated a real understanding of the pieces, others proved to be very clumsy.
Worse still: when, in 1802–03, the Sainte-Chapelle was fitted out to hold the archives of the Palais de Justice, the bottoms of all the windows were shortened by about 1.5 metres for the installation of cupboards.
The restorers thus had a huge job ahead of them; it would test their skills on different levels. First off, the medieval technique of glass painting had become obsolete during the 17th century and had to be rediscovered. Scientific research was carried out.
Then the entire iconography was to be redone. The archaeologist Ferdinand François de Guilhermy (1809–1878) accepted the difficult task of carrying out the necessary study to give sense back to the ensemble. The result is impressive and, despite a few uncertainties, similar to the initial programme.

The stained-glass windows of the choir and the prophetic cycle

The stained-glass windows of the choir are dedicated to a theological exposition of the Christian faith, focusing on the Passion of Christ, which occupies the central window, above the relics gallery. The narrative is introduced by that of the Childhood (left of centre), which recounts the Incarnation of Christ from the Annunciation (below) to the Massacre of the Innocents at the top of the lancet.
On either side, the stained-glass windows present the four great prophets who announced the events of the New Testament: Isaiah, Daniel, Ezekiel, and Jeremiah, joined by John the Baptist, the last prophet of the Old Testament, and John, the prophet of the Apocalypse.
The Isaiah window—the second on the left from the central window—is divided into two lancets: on the left, the life of the prophet and, on the right, the Jesse Tree, the most famous of his prophecies, which announced the coming of the Son of God. From the side of the patriarch Jesse, sleeping at the bottom, springs a stem whose stylised branches of leaves delineate a series of superimposed compartments in which are seated kings; then come the Virgin and Christ, surrounded by doves, symbols of the gifts of the Holy Spirit. On either side of these figures are the prophets who announced the Incarnation.
This composition, developed by Abbot Suger at the royal abbey of Saint-Denis, transposed into stained glass an idea that was important in medieval thought: the unction that the king receives during the coronation makes him God's vicar on earth, that is to say, his substitute, and therefore to depict the genealogy of the ancestors of Christ is to depict that of the Capetian kings who were their successors.

The stained-glass windows of the nave and the historical programme

The royal theme dominates in the stained-glass windows of the nave and up to the choir entrance, with the representation of the history of the chosen people, from the creation of the world until Louis IX himself. The accent is placed on the historical and institutional origins of the royalty and, at the same time, on the qualities of a king, his valour in defending the faith and his rejection of all forms of idolatry. The western rose window brings this development to an end with the Apocalypse, which evokes the end of time.
Such an exposition corresponds to the ideology current in the 13th century, which was based on a conception of history influenced by theologians and jurists. Founded on renewed study of the Bible, it demonstrated the continuity of the royal line by making it date back to earliest antiquity to the kings of Judah and Israel. The demonstration was of great interest to the monarchy during a period when the legitimation of any institution—especially the monarchy—rested on the authority of a long established tradition. Furthermore, Louis IX demonstrated his attachment to the ancientness of the French monarchy in another site, equally symbolic for the dynasty: the abbey of Saint-Denis. In 1263–64, the kings commissioned a series of tombs for all his ancestors going back to Dagobert. This ambitious funerary programme appeared to be the pendant of that of the Sainte-Chapelle.

The Gallery with the Great Reliquary in the Choir of the Upper Chapel, engraving by Charles Nicolas Ransonnette, for Sauveur Jérôme Morand, *Histoire de la Sainte-Chapelle royale du Palais* (Paris: chez Clousier et Prault, 1790).

Jean de Joinville offers his book to Louis, king of Navarre, future Louis X le Hutin (Louis the Stubborn), great-grandson of Saint Louis, manuscript from *La Vie de Saint Louis* (BNF, Paris, Mss, ms. fr. 13568, f° 1).

In the stained-glass windows of the upper chapel, the narrative begins with the Book of Genesis, in the window beside the north façade; this work, often repaired, is almost entirely a 19th-century creation. It is followed, going eastwards, by Exodus, Numbers, and the Book of Joshua. The first stained-glass window when entering the choir tells the story of the Judges, which links it to the historical cycle. The window facing it in the south of the choir dedicates a lancet to the story of Tobias, a model of filial piety who inspired Saint Louis. This text, with the books of Judith, Esther, and Job, formed the fifth part of the Bible of 1236. Here, they occupy the first two windows of the south side, from the choir. It should be noted that the story of Esther topped the niche where the queens stood—perhaps a tribute to the queen mother, Blanche. Did not the wife of Ahasuerus save her people like Blanche had safeguarded the kingdom of France?

Then there is the Book of Kings, dominated by the figure of David, the model of the pious king respectful of divine will—despite a few lapses. Finally, after this long section dedicated to the monarchy of Israel, there is one devoted to Louis IX, shown in his great act of piety: the purchase of the Holy Relics, their transport from Constantinople, their arrival in the kingdom, and then in Paris where they were presented. The three lower registers were devised by F. de Guilhermy to fill the gaps left by the removal of the cupboards; their iconography is thus uncertain.

This window rests on the west façade on which the end of time is evoked twice. And it should not be forgotten that the Christian king is accountable to God for leading his people to the end of time.

At the top of the western façade, the rose window of the Apocalypse details the vision of Saint John. The stained glass and stone architecture were changed in the late 15th century, but not the initial theme which relates the history of the Church, from its advent to the return of Christ and to the dreaded moment of the *Last Judgement*, represented on the tympanum of the portal of the upper chapel (redone in the 19th century). Stained glass and sculpture complement each other perfectly: the stone takes up where the glass leaves off.

Indeed, while we separate the images according to the techniques used to produce them to make it easier to read them, it should be borne in mind that they were conceived as elements intended to illustrate a global vision.

*

For the present-day visitor of the Sainte-Chapelle, this story will sound like a distant echo of a bygone era, whose points of reference seem to be a long way from our own. It accompanied the fortunes and misfortunes of the French monarchy with which it was identified for the same reasons as Reims, the cathedral where kings were crowned. The Sainte-Chapelle survived the events that marked the end of the Ancien Régime and the revolutionary period. But this survival was accompanied by a very profound change in meaning: it became the perfect symbol of Rayonnant Gothic architecture. The great restoration of the 19th century, however remarkable it may have been, completed the process of deconsecration begun in the Enlightenment. Religious ceremonies, held for a time for the reopening of the neighbouring Palais de Justice, are now limited to the mass of the feast day of Saint Ivo, the patron of lawyers, on 19 May.

The enthusiasm shown by Jean de Jandun in the 14th century will allow the contemporary visitor to see past the restored state and picture the Sainte-Chapelle as it was in its initial glory. So we will leave the last word to him:

"The carefully chosen colors of its paintings, the precious gilding of its images, the pure transparency of the stained glass that shines on all sides, the rich adornments of its altars, the marvellous virtues of its sanctuaries, the exotic ornaments of its reliquary shrines decorated with dazzling precious stones, give to that house of prayer such a degree of beauty that upon entering it one believes oneself carried up to the heavens, and one with reason believes oneself to be introduced into one of the most beautiful rooms of paradise."

Jean de Jandun, *A Treatise of the Praises of Paris*, 1323
Edited and translated by Robert W. Berger, *In Old Paris*, 8.

A CLOSER LOOK

On its north side, the Sainte-Chapelle overlooks the Cour de Mai, closed by the imposing mass of the Palais de Justice. This layout dates to the late 18th century.

The monument appears in its entirety in this old photograph (1968).
The counterforts, which reinforce the walls, are clearly visible on the south flank. Thicker at the base, they become narrower by successive steps to the level of the roof where they end in pinnacles. They give a vertical rhythm that lightens the massive appearance of the construction.
On the side of the western façade, the buttressing is provided by the terraces, corresponding to the two floors of the Sainte-Chapelle, and by the counterforts that frame them. The two staircase turrets on the corners of the façade now allow circulation between the two levels. The spire, rebuilt in 1853, dominates the roof.

Following pages

The lead structure in the foreground, on the left, is meant to hold the monumental angel on the eastern end of the roof. The masks of eight kings comprise the lower corolla. The western façade of Notre-Dame dominates the horizon of the modern city. In the 13th century, the cathedral, seat of the bishop of Paris, constituted the religious focus of the Île de la Cité, opposite the king in his palace.

The current spire, built between 1853 and 1855, is the fifth one to grace the roof of the Sainte-Chapelle. The angels at the bottom of the point sound trumpets or hold Instruments of the Passion of Christ. Gilded fleurs-de-lis are strewn over its sides.

At the base of the spire, where it joints the roof, the sculptor Adolphe Victor Geoffroy-Dechaume executed statues of the apostles bearing the instruments of their martyrdom. Saint Bartholomew, in the foreground, holds a cutlass and his skin and, to the right, Saint James the Less leans on a fuller's club.

The portal of the lower chapel, dedicated to the Virgin Mary, is decorated by the *Coronation of the Virgin* on the tympanum and the standing Virgin holding the Child on the pier. These works date from the 19th-century restoration and were produced by the studio of the sculptor Geoffroy-Dechaume. Only the embrasures preserve some of the medieval elements in the decoration of the small columns.

The lower chapel comprises a nave ending in the east with a seven-sided chevet, the whole surrounded by a very narrow ambulatory. In the central nave, each bay, square in plan, is arched by a ribbed vault whose key is at the same height as the bays of the ambulatory. This layout provides a solid base for the upper chapel. Strutting reinforces the very high transverse arches of the ambulatory.
The entire decoration was reconstituted by restorers in the 19th century: the polychromy of the vault and the columns, the stained-glass windows, and the tombstones of the canons, visible in the foreground.

The chevet of the lower chapel is lit by windows with two lancets. The stained-glass windows date from the 19th century. The two black columns, in the centre, are reinforcements added to support the relics gallery of the upper chapel. This photograph allows us to appreciate the polychromy: the ribs of the vaults, the window frames, the upper part of the arcade as well as the sculpted vegetation on the capitals have been gilded. The column in the foreground, on the left, bears the arms of Queen Blanche of Castile: *gules with castles of Castile or*. The darker small columns, visible in the blind arcade at the back of the choir, bear the arms of France: *azure with fleurs-de-lis or*.

Discovered in 1849 in the lower chapel, this mural is the only surviving trace of the 13th-century decoration. It decorates a blind window located at the left end of the choir and represents the *Annunciation* in the lancets and the *Virgin and Child* in the oculus of the tympanum. Its composition imitates that of a stained-glass window.

Following pages

The upper chapel greets the visitor with scintillating light and colours. The skill of the Gothic builders enabled them to reduce the masonry to the blind arcade running along the base of the windows and to the vaults, which rest on piers. The vividly coloured stained-glass windows constitute translucent walls that transform the Sainte-Chapelle into a vast reliquary.
Unlike the lower chapel, the space is unified; there is no ambulatory. The nave comprises four bays with rectangular plans, lit by large windows with four lancets, and ends in a seven-sided choir with windows with two lancets. The absence of furniture makes this nave—20.5 metres high—very impressive. The various elements of the monumental decoration (sculpture, painting, stained glass) combine to give a meaning to the whole.

The relics gallery, installed in the choir before 1267, housed the reliquary containing the great relics. The present layout was recreated using old fragments that had been retrieved. The central element of this complex structure is a raised platform supported by a pointed arch. It is topped by a baldachin, housing the altar with arches that corresponds to the position of the great reliquary. The gallery is accessed by two spiral staircases on either side.

The intrados of the arch supporting the relics gallery is adorned with two angels bearing, in their veiled hands, the Crown of Thorns. These sculptures date from the 19th-century restoration.

An angel with spread wings, hands clasped, in the right spandrel of the arch supporting the relics gallery. On the intrados, angels surrounded by the clouds hold the Instruments of the Passion of Christ—this one holds the nails. The painted decoration, restored in the 19th century, largely features the arms of France and Castile.

Each bay of the nave is flanked by two piers, which are buttressed on the exterior by counterforts. It comprises a stone-built portion, which forms the base for a large window with four lancets.
In the second bay from the choir on the south side of the nave, a niche made in the thickness of the wall interrupts the rhythm of the blind arcade. This is where the queens stood during the services. As the Queen Mother, Blanche of Castile, played a crucial role in helping Louis IX, she is particularly honoured here: the stained-glass window over the niche recounts the story of Esther, a queen who has saved her people, and the arms of Castile are inscribed in independent panels.

The blind arcade that runs along the chapel features quatrefoils depicting the martyrdoms of many saints. Here, the martyrdom of Saint Sebastian, repainted in the 19th century, stands out against an embossed and gilded ground.
In the spandrels between the arches, angels sculpted in low relief hold the crowns that honour the martyr saints.

There is sculpture everywhere. The flora that blossoms on the capitals invites divine creation into the religious space. This detail, from the blind arcade, shows a bird pecking at bouquets of oak, fig, and wormwood. The leaves, gilded and edged with a dark line, are treated realistically and stand out against a blue ground. The colours were reinstated by the 19th-century restorers.

Twelve figures of apostles stand against the piers that support the vault. Extensively damaged in 1802–03, when the Sainte-Chapelle was transformed into an archive for the Palais de Justice, they were recreated using pieces gathered in various places during the 19th-century restoration; the consoles beneath their feet as well as the canopies above their heads had been entirely redone. The identification of each of them is very uncertain as the attributes, which recall their martyrdom, were restored without great accuracy. With the martyrs evoked in the painted quatrefoils, they represent the Universal Church. Each figure holds a disc marked with a cross: these crosses recall the consecration of the Sainte-Chapelle and evoke the crusade that the king was preparing to embark upon.

Left-hand page

This apostle, one of the best preserved, is traditionally identified as Saint James the Less. Despite the layer of paint, the quality of the drapery is appreciable: the fullness of the garments heralds the style that would mark the second half of the 13th century.

Opposite left

This young and beardless apostle corresponds to the physical type of Saint John the Evangelist. The figure is draped in a simple cloak over a tunic that allows his feet to be seen.

Opposite right

This apostle, standing against the pier of the nave on the south side between the windows of Esther and the Kings, has not been identified. He is in different style from the two previous figures and yet he is contemporaneous with them.

Looking westwards, the visitor sees the part of the upper chapel that was the most greatly modified over the years. The rose window was entirely redone—tracery and stained glass—after 1485 in the Flamboyant Gothic style.

The decoration of the back of the western façade was devised by the 19th-century restorers. In 1856 Louis Steinheil was commissioned to paint, in the tympanum of the door, this representation of Christ, sitting on a throne with a baldachin, surrounded by angels holding candles or swinging thuribles. In the quatrefoils, he placed the figures of the prophets Isaiah and Jeremiah.

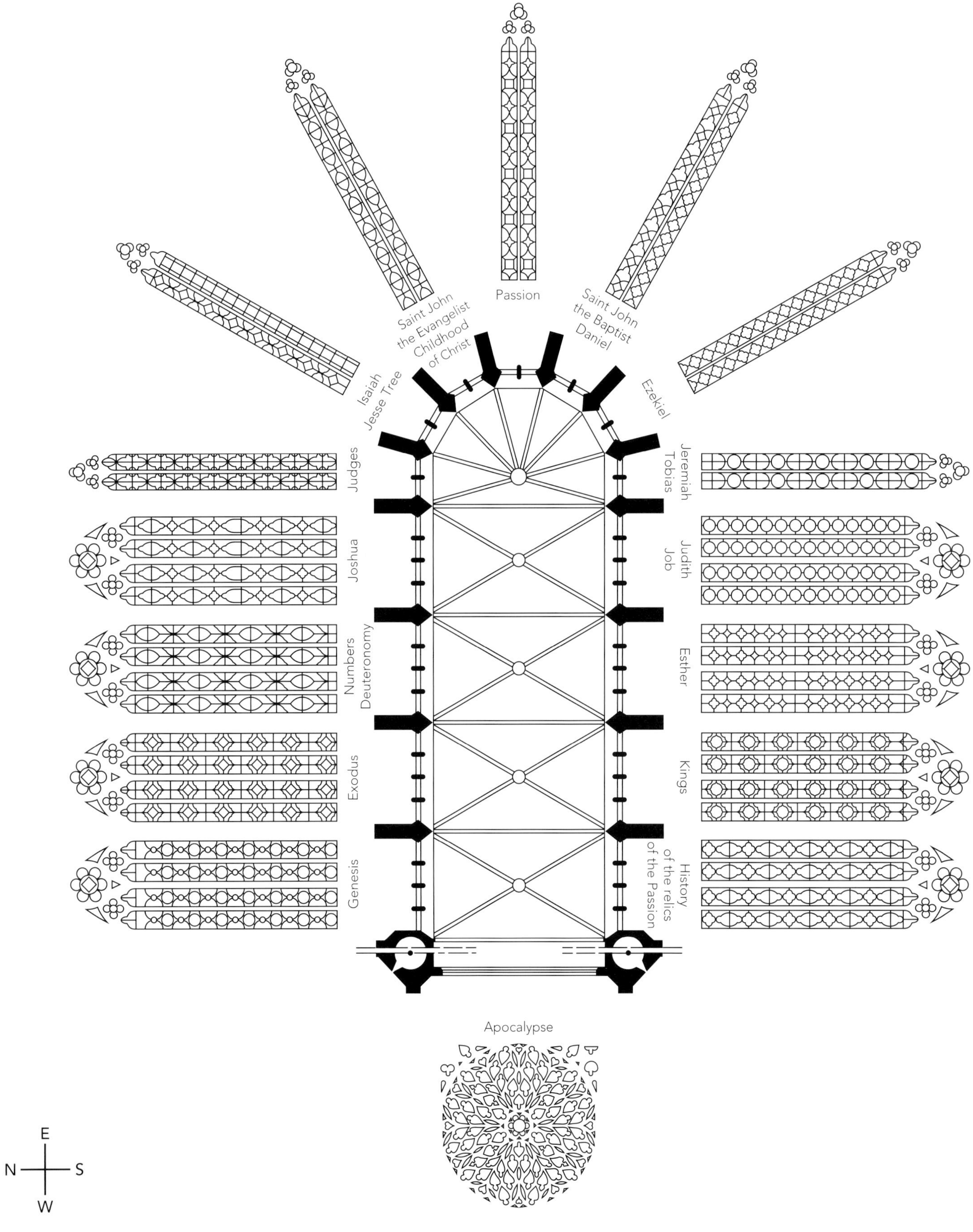
Passion
Saint John the Evangelist Childhood of Christ
Saint John the Baptist Daniel
Isaiah Jesse Tree
Ezekiel
Judges
Jeremiah Tobias
Joshua
Judith Job
Numbers Deuteronomy
Esther
Exodus
Kings
Genesis
History of the relics of the Passion
Apocalypse
E
N
S
W

In the present state of the monument, it is the interpretation of the stained-glass windows that allows the outline of the royal programme undertaken in the Sainte-Chapelle to be drawn out. And yet many uncertainties remain because of the successive restorations up to the modern era. The restoration overseen by Ferdinand François de Guilhermy around 1850 has the merit of having given the whole a stylistic unity in the spirit of the 13th century. In each stained-glass window, the overall composition is given by panels whose shape is determined by the fittings—quatrefoil squares, quatrefoils, elongated quatrefoils—as can be seen here in the windows of the south side. Each panel corresponds to a scene. For the most part, they may be read from bottom to top and from left to right in successive registers.

The window at the centre of the choir, to the left of the photograph, illustrates the Passion of Christ, whose relics are found in the relics gallery, located immediately above it. The window to the right belongs to the prophetic cycle. The story of Saint John the Baptist, the last prophet of the Old Testament, is told in the left lancet, and that of Daniel, one of the four great prophets, in the right lancet.

The scene of the Coronation of Thorns, in a square compartment, belongs to the window of the Passion: a green crown of thorns is placed on the head of Christ, haloed in red with a white cross. He is seated in the centre and his executioners mock him by acclaiming him king. The identical composition is found in the Numbers window. Note the half-red, half-yellow garment, which designates a villain, here an executioner.

These two windows are in the north part of the choir. The window close to the centre, with almond-shaped compartments, is divided into the Childhood of Christ, in the right lancet, and the story of Saint John the Evangelist, the prophet of the Apocalypse, in the other. The window on the left is entirely dedicated to the prophet Isaiah. The left lancet illustrates the life of the prophet, that on the right, his most famous prophecy, the Jesse Tree.

The upper part of the Jesse Tree. Among the prophecies of Isaiah, the theologians of the Middle Ages gave a special place to the coming of Christ, in the lineage of Jesse, the father of King David. Its representation in the form of a family tree gave it its title. Above all, these Old Testament kings were considered ancestors of the kings of France whose coronations elevated them to the rank of vicars of Christ. The Sainte-Chapelle window depicts fourteen kings. Each is seated in the centre of a compartment made of the branches of the tree and is flanked by prophets who announced the good news. This register is repeated fourteen times. In the upper section, the two registers above the last king contain the Virgin, then Christ. The two last panels show, in the plant scrolls, the doves that symbolise the gifts of the Holy Spirit.

Detail of the following view. A man, at the top of a castle, blows a horn. Note how the medieval image was inspired by everyday life—here in the evocation of the castle with its crenellated walls.

The three registers reproduced here belong to the Numbers window. This book of the Old Testament recounts everything related to the legal and religious organisation of the tribes of Israel. In the lower panel on the left, the interior of the tabernacle is depicted with a seven-branched candelabrum in the centre and, on the left, the Ark of the Covenant. The two panels above illustrate an interview between Moses, identified by the horns of light that frame his forehead, and God, with a red halo with a white cross.

The Book of Numbers is particularly interested in the counting of the tribes of Israel and in the appointment of a leader at the head of each of them. Medieval thinkers interpreted these passages as the beginnings of the monarchy. The crowning of the princes of Israel is thus repeated in various guises—as in the eight panels reproduced here. This window is located above the niche where the king stood when he came to the Sainte-Chapelle: he thus showed himself to be the descendant of these distant ancestors. The royal character of the window is accentuated by the pattern of gold fleurs-de-lis on an azure ground, which are the arms of France—to which are joined those of Blanche of Castile.

The stained-glass window whose upper section we see here recounts the story of Joshua, the designated heir of Moses, and, in the upper rose, that of Ruth and Boaz. It lights the last bay of the nave, on the north side, before entering the choir. The composition is representative of the 13th century: the shape of the historiated compartments is determined by the fittings; they stand out against a decorative ground; a thin border makes a link with the tracery of the window.

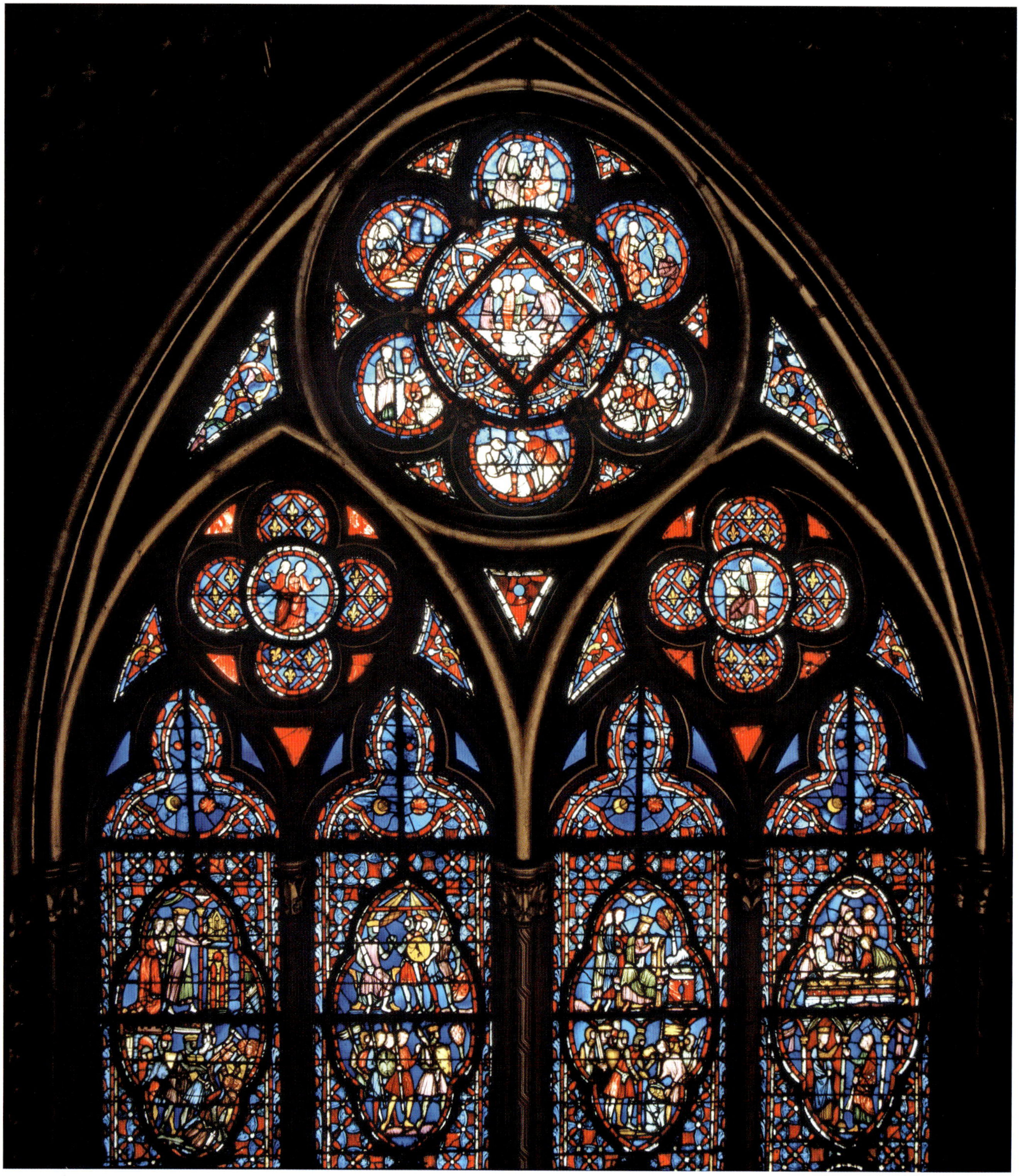

In these panels from the Joshua window, note the lengthening of the upper half of the two large quatrefoils: the glassworkers adjusted the shape of the panels so as to take into account a metal truss rod that encircles the entire Sainte-Chapelle to reinforce its stability. In the scene of the top left, the walls of the city of Jericho collapse as men blow horns. On the right, Joshua kneeling in from of an altar offers the spoils of his conquest.

The story of Joshua is that of the conquest of the Promised Land. There were thus many cavalcades. In the panel reproduced here, the Amorean kings flee from Joshua. These scenes herald the crusade that King Louis IX was preparing to embark upon towards the Holy Land. The horsemen wearing coats of mail are armed like 13th-century knights.

These four registers of scenes belong to the Judges window. This window has undergone major restorations—for example, the panel on the upper left where Samson combats the lion was redone in the 19th century. The scenes that concern Jephthah's daughter are quite well-preserved. In the second register from the bottom on the left, two girls, dancing, welcome the return of the victorious soldiers to victory led by their chief Jephthah. But he had promised to sacrifice the first girl who came to meet him: he despaired when he recognised his own daughter. In the quatrefoil on the bottom to the right, she weeps with her companions while awaiting execution (lower panel) and an executioner prepares to behead her (scene above).

This detail of the window of Judith depicts the sadness of the people after the death of the heroine who, by killing Holophernes, delivered her people. The scene is located in a religious building comprising a series of arches delimiting three bays. In each bay, a lamp hangs. A pink roof appears behind the two arches on the right, which rest on columns with capitals with crockets—as in 13th century architecture. Ahead of these two bays with red backgrounds lies Judith's coffin. Under a white gable topping a blue background, men make gestures of grief. Below the scene, a black-painted band bears an inscription in white letters left in reserve, which reads: "CI : PLEVRE LA MORT" (here, the death [of Judith] is grieved). The use of the vernacular language in the Sainte-Chapelle demonstrates the independence of the king with regard to the religious authorities that favoured the use of Latin.

The upper section of the window of Judith leaves room for the story of Job, a model of piety particularly revered during the Middle Ages.

When the ordeals descended upon him, Job had had his hair cut. He is sitting on a blue and yellow bench, in his house suggested by a set of architectural elements—two side doors with a red ground linked by a crenellated white wall above a blue ground. A servant stands in front of him and seizes a lock of hair with shears (large scissors of the 13th century).

One of the ordeals Job had to face was losing his children: while they were feasting, the house collapsed on them. At the top of the panel, a green devil pushes elements of the architecture onto the young people. To imitate bleeding wounds, the glass painters used irregular pieces of red glass.

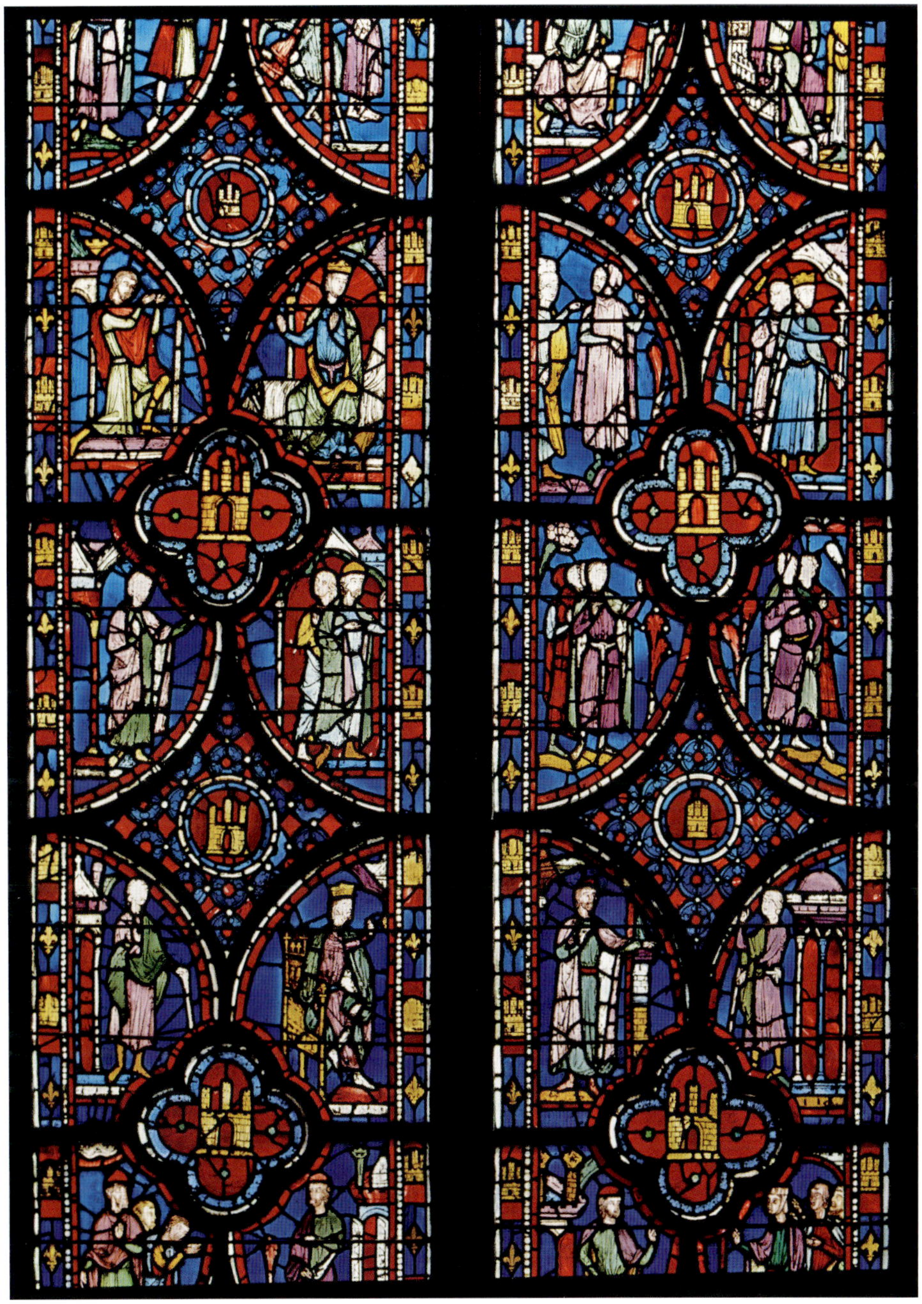

Details of the Esther window. These two panels match each other above the mullion that separates the third and fourth lancet, in three registers, at the top of the stained-glass window. King Ahasuerus, with the insignia of his function—crown and sceptre—is sitting in a throne chair decorated with balusters and receives Esther, who kneels before him, on the right. Each figure is placed underneath a white gable—inspired by the contemporary architecture of the Sainte-Chapelle.

The second window of the nave on the south side, starting from the choir, recounts the story of Esther, the Jewish wife of King Ahasuerus, who would save her people. This window is placed above the niche where Queen Blanche of Castile attended the services. It pays emphatic tribute to the king's mother: the independent quatrefoils display the arms of the queen.

This scene is from the Kings window. Bathsheba, half-immersed in a green tub, is bathing. She speaks to her servant, standing on the left, who pours water into the bathtub.

The Kings window gives pride of place to the story of King David. The episodes represented are in the first two lancets, under the third register of quatrefoil squares. They evoke David's youth and his first exploits. In the quatrefoil square of the right lancet, David brings the head of Goliath to King Saul—this scene is heavily restored but follows the initial composition.

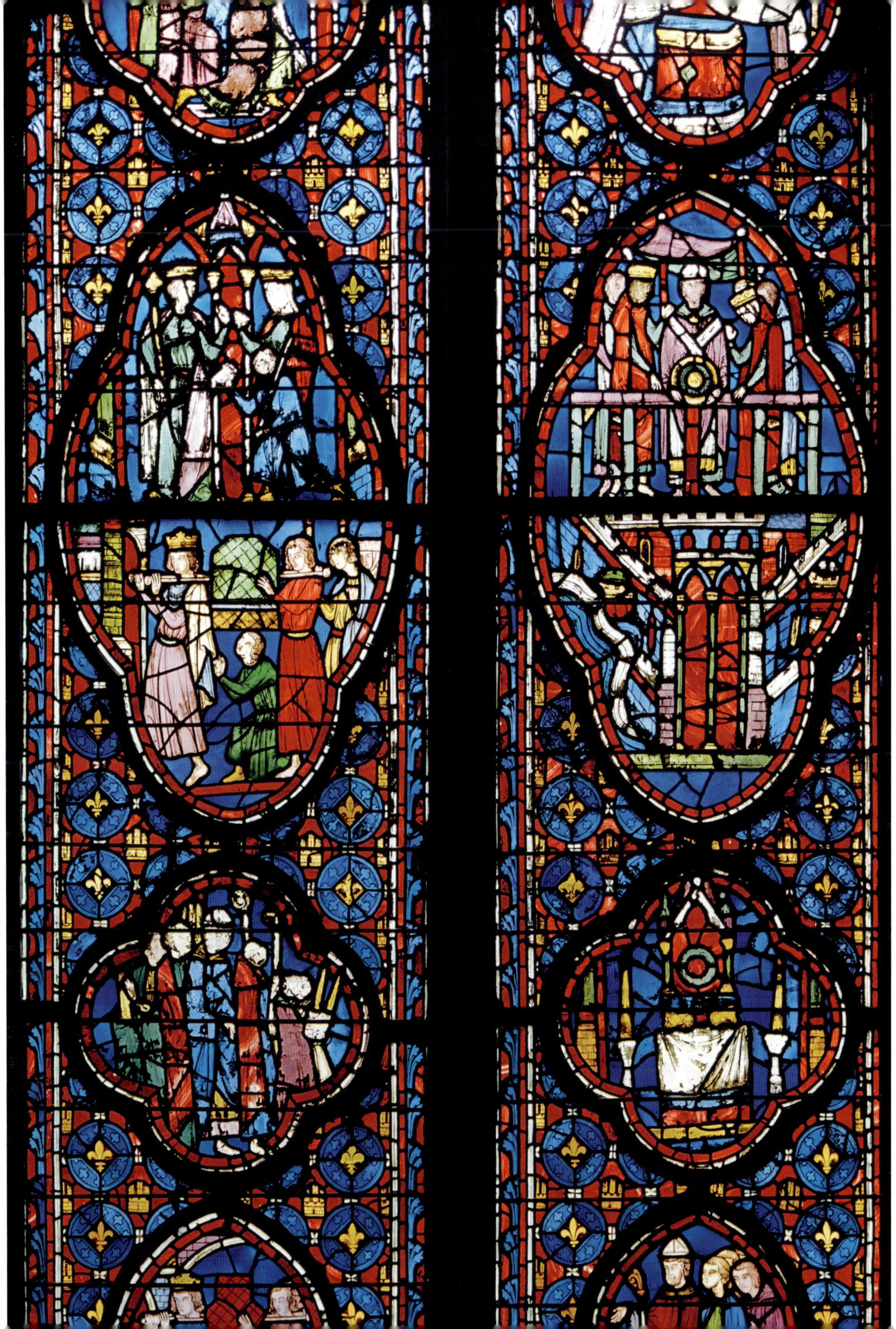

The last window on the south side, adjoining the façade, is dedicated to King Louis IX. The founder of the Sainte-Chapelle takes his place after King David in the lineage of Old Testament kings. He is depicted in his most wonderful act of piety accomplished so far: the purchase of the relics of the Passion.
In the elongated quatrefoil, in the upper right of the image, he is present alongside the archbishop of Sens for the showing of the Holy Crown.
His mother, Queen Blanche, recognisable because of her widow's wimple, is also present.
The scene takes place in Paris, in the Île de la Cité, which figures in the lower half of the same quatrefoil.
In the small quatrefoil of the right lancet, the Crown of Thorns is presented on an altar, under a canopy—as it would be a little later on the relics gallery.

Small quatrefoil on the left lancet of the window of Louis IX.
The king and his brother Robert d'Artois carry on their shoulders the reliquary containing the holy relics. They are about to enter a city represented in the background—Sens or Paris. It should be noted that, on this window, the king is always depicted wearing his crown, but never haloed. He was not canonised until 1297.

Detail of the window of Louis IX.
In the lower half of the large quatrefoil at the top of the left lancet, the king carries the reliquary of the Cross in his veiled hands. He is followed by his mother, Queen Blanche. The procession is heading for the group of attendants standing in the panel of the neighbouring lancet.

The theme of the large rose window in the top of the western façade is the Apocalypse.
This vision of the end of time, transcribed by Saint John, puts an end to the New Testament.
The rose should be read as the continuation of the window of Louis IX whose duty as a Christian king was precisely to guide his people to this dreaded moment.
The present rose window was rebuilt in the late 15th century and replaces the original rose window, which treated the same subject. The composition is organised around the central oculus.

In the centre of the rose, Christ appears seated on the rainbow, the sword of speech going out of his mouth, surrounded by seven golden candlesticks and seven stars (Rev. 1: 12–16). He blesses Saint John, prostrated at his feet (Rev. 1: 17), in the lower left. In the other foils, small chapels with angels standing before them evoke the seven churches of Asia to which the message is addressed (Rev. 2 and 3). The painting on glass is very different from that of the 13th century used in the rest of the Sainte-Chapelle. The proportions are larger, the range of colours more extensive, and the painting more complex. It was henceforth possible to have several colours on the same piece of glass without separating them with a lead. For example, we see the silver stain belt that girds the chest of Christ over his white robe (Rev. 1: 13).

This part of the narrative is located in the left part of the rose window. The scene in the upper left refers to the story of the witnesses put to death then resurrected (Rev. 11: 3–13). On the right, the Elders bow down before God (Rev. 11: 15–16). Above these episodes, we recognize the woman "clothed with the sun" —surrounded by golden rays—who gives her child to an angel to save him from the dragon who appears in the lower left opening (Rev. 12: 3–6).

The two horsemen who appear in the left of the image belong to the first circle of the composition: one is armed with a bow and the second with a sword (Rev. 6: 2 and 4). In the centre of the image, the dragon with seven heads comes out of the sea; he is adored by the people, in the lower right, and pursues the woman who flees to the desert (Rev. 12: 13–14 and beginning of chapter 13).

The base of the portal of the upper chapel is decorated with scenes from Genesis, inscribed in quatrefoil squares and treated in low relief. On the lower register, to the left, Eve spins while Adam digs. Above, two episodes relating to Noah —the animals embark on the ark and the ark at sea. The fleurs-de-lis and the castles of Castile recall the patrons, Louis IX and his mother, Blanche of Castile.

The western portal allowed the king to enter the upper chapel directly from his apartments. This portal was entirely refurbished by the studio of the sculptor Geoffroy-Dechaume around 1850, styled on the decoration of the central door of neighbouring Notre-Dame Cathedral. On the tympanum is the *Last Judgement*: Christ, seated, shows the wounds in his hand, side, and feet. He is flanked by two angels who hold the Instruments of the Passion, the nails (on the left) and the cross (on the right). Kneeling on the sides are the Virgin and Saint John, imploring Christ to be merciful to those awaiting judgement. The lintel shows the latter coming out of their graves. On the pier, Christ holds the globe and gives a blessing.

IN DEPTH

The spire

The spire that tops the middle of the roof was rebuilt five times. The first was built at the same time as the rest of the building but, by the reign of Charles VI, the wood had rotted. In 1383 the master carpenter to the king, Robert Fouchier, undertook the building of the second spire in wood and lead. It may be seen in a miniature in *Les Très Riches Heures* painted by the Limburg brothers for the Duke of Berry in the early 15th century: it appears in the background of the haymaking scene that illustrates the month of June. In 1460, a sculptor from Tours, Guillaume Brassefort, was called on "to visit the steeple of the Sainte-Chapelle of the palace in the Cité . . . and negotiate about making several sculptures . . . around the spire" (Henri Stein, *Le Palais de Justice et la Sainte-Chapelle de Paris. Notice historique et archéologique* [Paris: D. A. Longuet, 1912], 123). Unfortunately, the terrible fire of 26 July 1630 destroyed the roof, along with the spire—the third. Arrangements were made with a view to its reconstruction, which was approved by King Louis XIII in 1634. Only, the work progressed slowly. The bells rang for the funeral service of Queen Anne of Austria, the mother of Louis XIV, in 1666, but the installation of the lead roof was not completed until 1671. The revolutionaries gave the death blow to this fourth spire, which was decorated with the royal crown, fleurs-de-lis, and the king's monogram—unbearable signs of feudalism. The invention to tender for the demolition took place on 7 August 1793. Thus came down to the 19th-century restorers the task of building a fifth spire, the one that we see today. They decided to have the work done in the spirit of the 15th century. The sculptor Geoffroy-Dechaume executed the sculpture for it. This building project had lasting success: several of the buildings restored after the Sainte-Chapelle were given a spire in the same style, beginning with Notre-Dame de Paris.

The Sainte-Chapelle with its Spire between 1583 and 1587 by Jacques Cellier, drawing on paper, 16th century (BNF, Paris, Mss, ms. fr. 9152, f. 89).

Sketch of three statues of angels for the ornamentation of the spire, pencil drawing on paper by Geoffroy-Dechaume, 19th century (CAPA, Paris, Fonds Geoffroy-Dechaume, DSS 30).

Statues of four angels of the Passion for the base of the spire, photograph on salted paper by the Bisson brothers, 1853 (CAPA, Paris, Fonds Geoffroy-Dechaume, PH 92).

The restoration of the polychromy and the paintings

Statue of one of the apostles. Polychrome sculpture, 19th century (MAP, Charenton-le-Pont).

What strikes the visitor entering the Sainte-Chapelle is the atmosphere created by the saturated colours. This is due to the painted polychromy on all the elements of the masonry, from the walls to the vaults, intensified in the upper chapel by the coloured light of the stained glass.

Originally, the two levels of the Sainte-Chapelle were certainly painted, and fairly substantial traces remained at least in the top sections of the upper chapel, which were less affected by the transformations. The architect Félix Duban carefully made drawings of them before beginning the restoration. However, it was not until 1841 that it was agreed in principle to restore the building in colour. To get an idea of the effect, the restoration was applied in a bay of the upper chapel. At the top of the gilded arcade, scenes of martyrdom were repainted in the quatrefoil medallions; the bottom of one of the arches was decorated, as an example, with a geometric motif; the piers supporting the statues of the apostles were given a heraldic decoration—a pattern of gold fleurs-de-lis on azure for the king and *gules* (red in heraldic language) with gold castles of Castile for Queen Blanche of Castile; the apostles themselves were painted; the starting point of the stained glass was drawn above the arcade in such as way as to highlight the point where it meets the windows. There were multiple delays and this part of the restoration extended into the 1860s.
The organ was located at the back of the western façade. The last one, built by François Henri Cliquot, had been installed in 1762. Taken down during the Revolution, it is now in the church of Saint-Germain-l'Auxerrois. Its departure left the wall empty. In 1856, the architects entrusted to the cartoon painter Louis Steinheil the creation of the new decoration, inspired in part by the Psalter of Saint Louis in the Bibliothèque Nationale de France (Département des Manuscrits, ms. lat. 10525).
The works on the polychromy of the entire building also included the restoration of the paving stones. It was the architect Émile Boeswillwald (1815–1896) who had the hardstone paving stones, inlaid with various motifs, installed.

A bird, detail of the paving restored under the supervision of the architect Émile Boeswillwald (MAP, Charenton-le-Pont).

Paintings of the Sainte-Chapelle, detail of the polychromy of the Sainte-Chapelle drawn by the architect Charles Percier (1764–1838) (Bibliothèque de l'Institut de France, Paris, ms. 1012, f. 50).

The restoration of the stained-glass windows

The restoration of the stained-glass windows, begun in 1845, posed specific iconographic, aesthetic, and technical problems. Only the upper chapel was concerned as there have been no stained-glass windows in the lower chapel since the flood of 1690.
The cupboards, installed from 1802 onwards to house the archives of the neighbouring Palais de Justice, had encroached upon the windows in such a way that two or three registers of scenes had been walled up in each of them. There were two possible solutions for filling in the gaps: either to leave the windows without their (walled-up) lower sections or to complete them with new scenes. The second was chosen, and the archaeologist Ferdinand François de Guilhermy (1809–1878) was put in charge of finding the meaning of each stained-glass window and of creating complementary scenes.
As for the question of aesthetics, this was linked to the general state of the glass. In accordance with the will of Saint Louis, the stained-glass windows were maintained regularly, but five centuries of interventions had modified the overall appearance: the restorations, more or less respectful, had introduced, over the years, elements that too often contrasted with the original pieces. After much deliberation, it was decided, in the name of the unity of style already invoked for the polychromy and for the sculpture, to restore all the stained-glass windows to their 13th-century appearance—with the exception of the rose window, rebuilt and glazed in the late 15th century.
This decision implied the quest for a certain technical mastery. In the 17th and 18th centuries, classical architecture had so much kept its distance from glass painting that this skill had become obsolete.
A competition was thus organised to select a glass painter capable of painting in the manner of the 13th century. In the first place, the processes of manufacturing coloured glass like the old glass had to be found. As it was a period of scientific rationalisation, chemists joined in on the research. The red glass posed particular problems that the glassmaker Georges Bontemps (1801–1882) overcame at the Choisy-le-Roi glassworks in 1836.
A stained-glass window in the church of Saint-Germain-l'Auxerrois, dated 1839, is a souvenir of these trials: it features the copy of panels after the window of the Passion at the Sainte-Chapelle.
The cartoon painter Louis Steinheil (1814–1885), who took over this project in 1845, had full-scale drawings done of all the panels of the upper chapel. They bear witness to the great accuracy of the work carried out in the studio of glass painter Antoine Lusson (1808?–1876).
These documents also allow us to spot that some of the panels have not been reincorporated, for different reasons.
For example, a cherub was excluded from the Judges window, as his wings were painted with silver stain, which dates him to after the construction of the Sainte-Chapelle, as the use of silver stain only began in the early 14th century.
Other panels, such as the scene in which the devils make Job's flocks flee, had been too heavily restored in the 15th century.
When the greatly altered scene was necessary to the iconographic development, the restorers refashioned in the style of the 13th century —such was the case for *David Presenting Goliath's Head to Saul*.
The general arrangement chosen certainly contributed greatly to the impression of "Gothic authenticity" felt by contemporary visitors.

Panel from the story of Job restored in the 15th century: the tree trunk with ivy and the coats of mail of the devils date from the 13th century, but the head of the devil in the centre, the dappled horse, and the shepherds were all redone during the restoration.

The Stained-Glass Windows of the Sainte-Chapelle, reproductions by Louis Steinheil, gouache on paper, c. 1850 (MAP, Charenton-le-Pont).

David presents the head of Goliath to King Saul in a scene from the Kings window. The drawing on the left shows the state of the panel before 1848: only some fragments of Saul's clothing and his chair date from the 13th century. The document on the right is the cartoon used by the glass painter to restore the original appearance of the scene.

Scattered artefacts

Reliquary of the Holy Crown now in the treasury of Notre-Dame de Paris. It was designed by the architect Jules Godefroy Astruc and executed by the goldsmith Maurice Poussielgue-Rusand.

A visit to the Sainte-Chapelle can be prolonged by other, more or less distant excursions. The Crown of Thorns has found refuge in Notre-Dame Cathedral where it may be seen in the treasury. Moreover, it is offered up to the prayers of the congregation the first Friday of the month and every Friday during Lent.
The lovely ivory Virgin (*c.* 1265), mentioned in the first inventory of the treasury, has become part of the Department of Decorative Arts at the Musée du Louvre, as have the large plaques of painted enamel, illustrating the Passion, that King Henri II and Queen Catherine de Médicis had commissioned to decorate the choir screen in 1552 from Léonard Limosin after drawings by Nicolo dell'Abate.
The Department of Sculptures also in the Louvre contains the *Pietà* by Germain Pilon, sculpted for Saint-Denis, but installed for a time in the upper chapel.
At the time it was founded (1843), the Musée de Cluny (the present Musée National du Moyen Âge-Thermes de Cluny) was used to store artefacts by the Monuments Historiques. It received various elements during the great restoration of the 19th century that can still be seen: architectural elements; sculptures of the apostles, whose state did not allow them to be returned to the Sainte-Chapelle; and stained-glass panels. Other objects entered the museum collections, including two mitres in particular.
The Musée National de la Renaissance at the Château d'Écouen, for its part, houses the altar of gilded wood, dating from the 1524, on which the great reliquary was placed.
The last organ, installed by Louis XVI, has found a home in the church of Saint-Germain-l'Auxerrois, which is opposite the Colonnade of the Louvre.
Two departments of the Bibliothèque Nationale de France watch over the surviving objects in the treasury of the Sainte-Chapelle.
The Department of Manuscripts contains books that may be admired during the exhibitions held by the establishment.
As for the Department of

Gilded wood altar that served as a base for the great reliquary, 1524 (Musée National de la Renaissance, Écouen).

The Crucifixion, in the centre, with scenes of the Passion and the portrait of King François I and Queen Claude de France, by Léonard Limosin. Enamel plaque destined for the choir screen of the Sainte-Chapelle, 1552 (Musée du Louvre, Paris, Department of Decorative Arts, MR XIII suppl.).

Tip of a cantoral staff. The attribute of the cantor, the second most important figure in the ecclesiastical college, was a staff whose tip featured an ornament. This one is an ancient cameo most likely representing Constantine (*c.* 315–330). It was mounted in this metalwork setting at the request of King Charles V between 1368 and 1377 (BNF, Paris, Cabinet des Médailles, Bab. 909).

Medals, it keeps close guard of the Great Cameo of France as well as the top of the staff, which is the insignia of the cantor. At the time when the archives of the Palais de Justice were placed there, the glazier hired to take down the stained-glass windows took them and sold them. This explains the presence of original panels of the Sainte-Chapelle in Rouen (Musée des Antiquités de la Seine-Maritime), Chalon-sur-Saône (Musée Vivant-Denon), and even the United Kingdom (Canterbury, Twycross, Wilton, and the Victoria and Albert Museum in London). A visit of the Sainte-Chapelle in Paris is therefore an invitation to a long journey.

The Great Cameo of France. Five-layered sardonyx cameo, Rome, *c.* ad 23. This large gem was mentioned in the first inventory of the Sainte-Chapelle (before 1279) (BNF, Paris, Cabinet des Médailles, Bab. 264).

Centre des monuments nationaux

President
Philippe Bélaval

Managing director
Bénédicte Lefeuvre

Éditions du patrimoine

Publishing director
Jocelyn Bouraly

Publications coordinator
Catherine Donzel

Editorial coordinator
Anne-Sophie Grouhel-Le Tellec

Translator
Chrisoula Petridis

Copy editor
Susan Schneider

Production coordinator
Carine Merse

Graphic design
Cyril Cohen
Régis Dutreuil

Photoengraving
APS-Chromostyle, Tours

Printing
IME, Baume-les-Dames, France

Abbreviations

BNF: Bibliothèque Nationale de France;
CAPA: Cité de l'Architecture et du Patrimoine;
MAP: Médiathèque de l'Architecture et du Patrimoine.

Dépôt légal: May 2013

ISBN: 978-2-7577-0271-0
ISSN: 1960-3304

Photographic credits

Bibliothèque Inguimbertine, Carpentras: 6
Bibliothèque de l'Institut de France, Paris/The Bridgeman Art Library/Archives Charmet: 64br
Bibliothèque municipale de Toulouse: 4tr
BNF, Paris: 5tl, 7tl and bl, 8tr, 9, 11, 16, 63t, 67tl and bl
Gérard Boulay: 66t
Cité de l'architecture et du patrimoine, Paris: 63bl and br
CMN / Bernard Acloque: 26, 29, 33, 34, 35t, 36, 37, 39, 42, 43, 44, 46, 47, 48, 49, 51, 52, 53, 54, 55, 56, 57, 58, 59, 60, 64tr
CMN / Philippe Berthé: 24, 25
CMN / David Bordes: front cover, 30-31, 35b, 38, 41
CMN / Patrick Cadet: 13, 15, 45, 50
CMN / Jean-Pierre Delagarde: 2, 20, 22-23, 32
CMN / Jean Feuillie: 21, 28, 61
CMN / Pascal Lemaître: 5bl, 27
CMN / MAP, Charenton-le-Pont: 4bl, 5br, 7br
CMN / Caroline Rose: 12, 65
Lechartier © Inventaire général du Patrimoine culturel de Haute-Normandie: 3
RMN / Daniel Arnaudet: 67r
RMN / Gérard Blot: 8tl, 66b

Cover illustration

The upper chapel.